SEE-SAW

A Sampler of *How Once We Looked*

SEEING NOW WHAT WE SAW BACK THEN

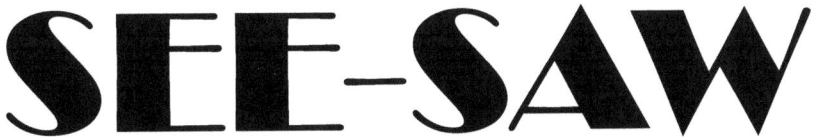
michael philip manheim

PHOTOGRAPHY

SEE-SAW

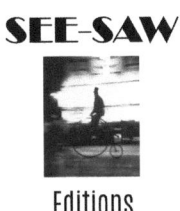

Editions

ALSO BY MICHAEL PHILIP MANHEIM

IN A LABYRINTH
LAST HOUSE STANDING
WHERE MY SPIRIT GUIDES US

Book design and layout: J. Putnam Design www.jputnamdesign.com

Printed in the United States of America.

ISBN 978-0-9844803-3-3

Cover photograph: *Little Sister*

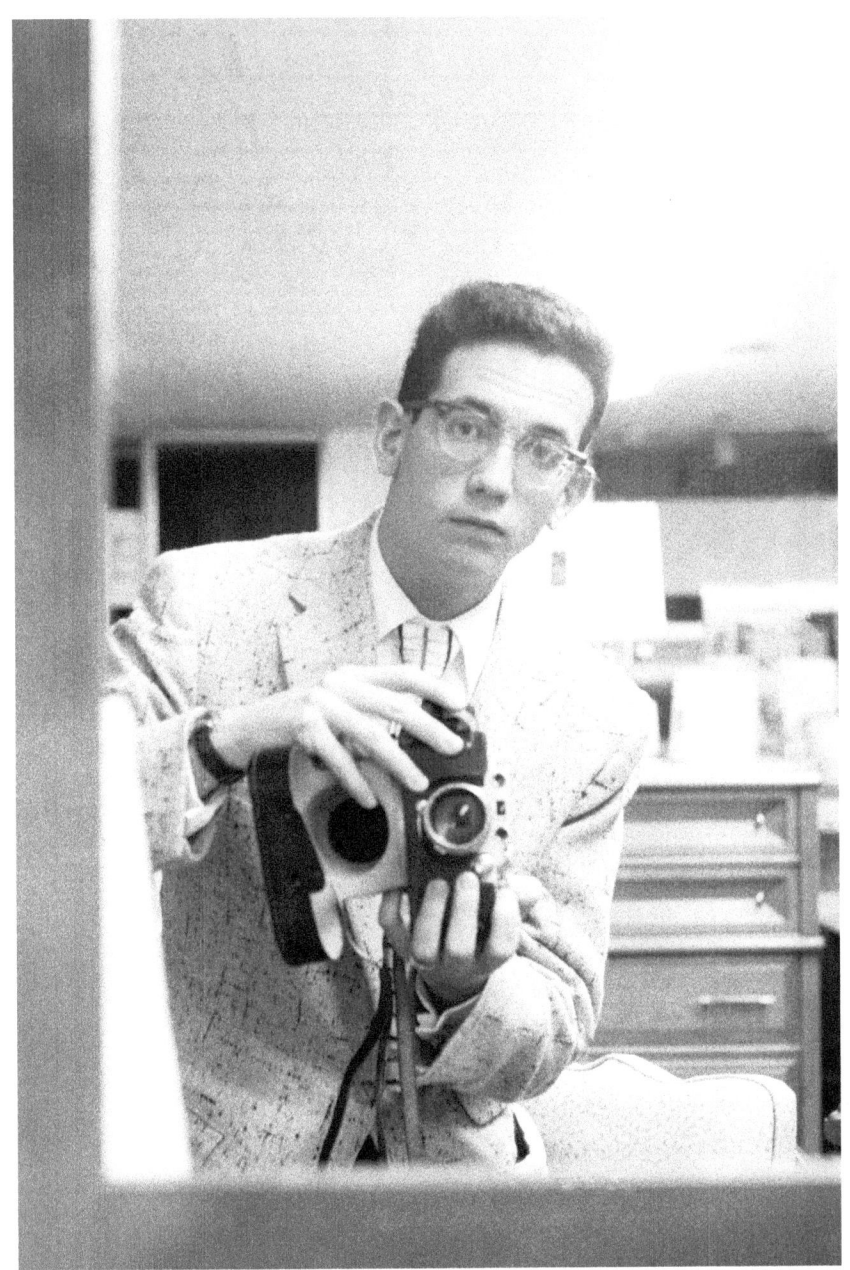

15 year-old Me *Alliance, Ohio 1956*

This series of my nostalgic photography books is dedicated to

Stephen B. Jareckie
Consulting Curator of Photography
at the Fitchburg Art Museum in Fitchburg, Massachusetts.

As Curator of Photography at the Worcester Art Museum, Stephen Jareckie
was the very first to welcome me into his world of fine art photography.

When it was timely to find my way among galleries and museums,
Stephen offered to take a look at what I was creating.
I was honored and enlightened. He gave me the tips that sent me on my way.
And he continued this mentoring.

Upon retiring from Worcester, Jareckie stayed in demand —
hence his work as consultant at the Fitchburg Art Museum.

Stephen has an encyclopedic understanding of photography's evolution,
and of the photographers whose works fostered that growth.
I continue to be appreciative of an expert so caring and giving,
and so refreshingly open to both nostalgia and new vision.

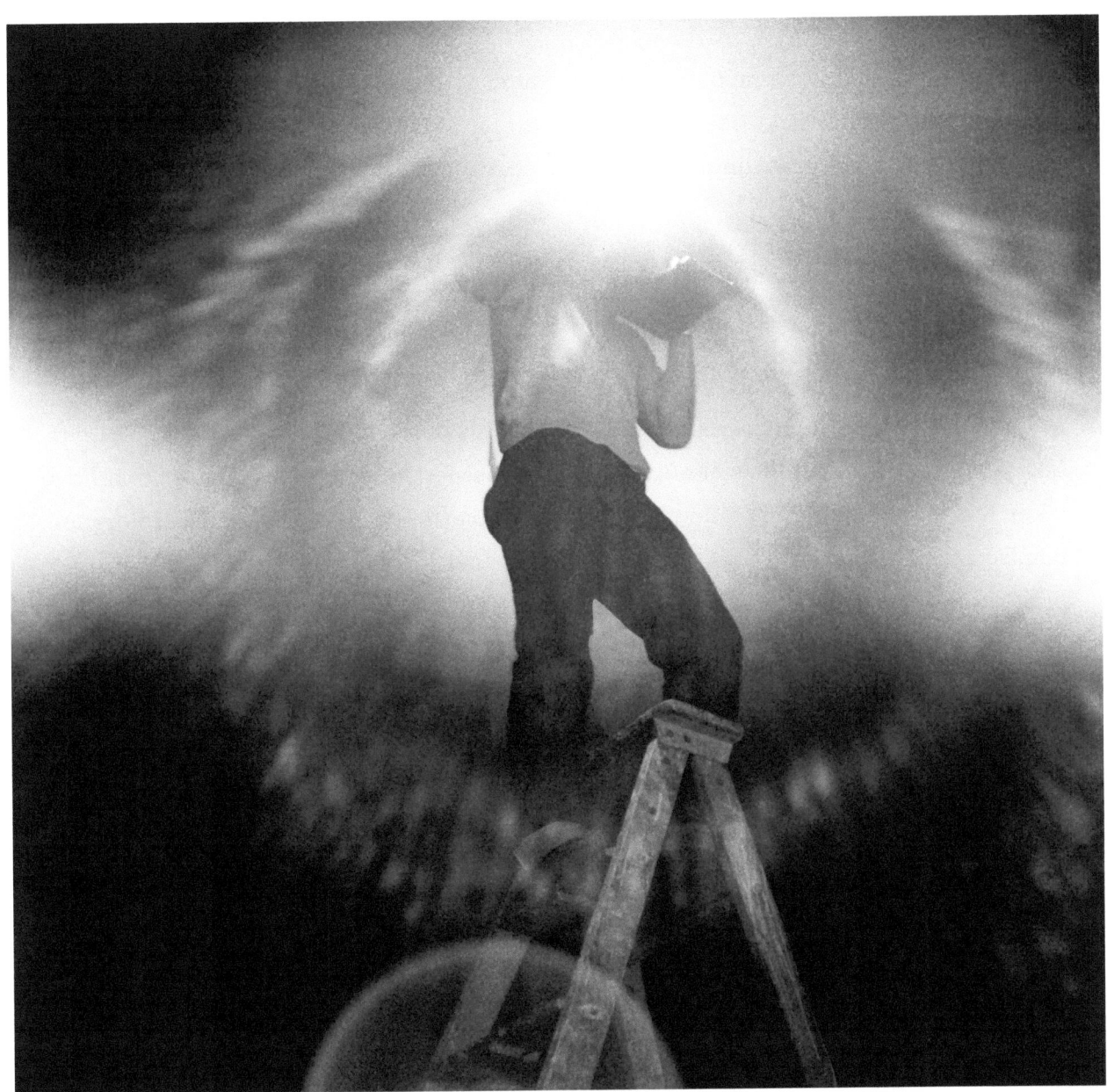

Flash! *Alliance, Ohio 1956*

Foreword

In the modern world of a million options for almost everything, it is a struggle to stand out and create something beautiful and different. This is particularly true in the arts; whether photography, writing, painting, music, or any other imaginable pursuit of the human spirit.

As an historian of the American Civil War, as well as a lover of photography (but with no talent for it) who instead tries to paint word pictures, I can appreciate the potential of innovative photography to create something original, meaningful, and important.

Not many photographers have been as daring in this pursuit as Michael Philip Manheim. Like any artist seeking the undefined, he has passed through many phases that have taken him to the frontier of photographic breakthrough. His multiple-image exploration, inspired by his quest to reveal feelings that he had long been intent on capturing in photojournalism, has been shown online and in books and exhibitions.

After years on his journey into the abstract Manheim, in this "little album" of photographs, has returned to his inspiration of early documentary works. "I am going into the archives," he says, "to see what I saw long ago." For us it is another journey to relish with this innovative photographer.

— John C. Waugh

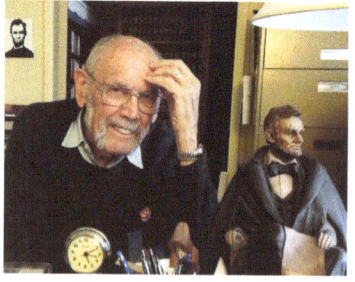

John C. Waugh concentrates on his own nostalgia as author of The Class of 1846 *and* Reelecting Lincoln, *among his one dozen books on the Civil War era. Waugh's extensive research draws upon actual historical writings, weaving them together into compelling narratives.*

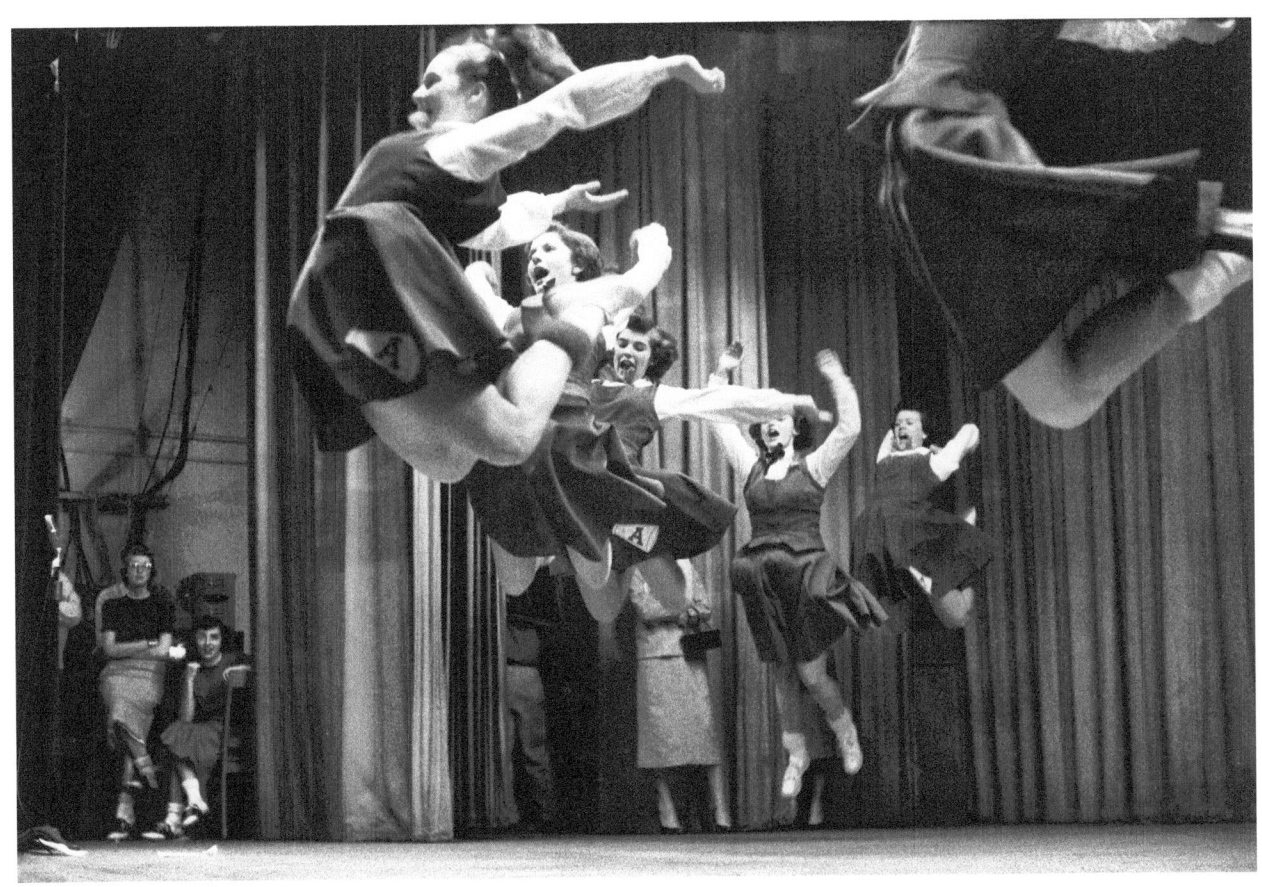

Ladies Leaping *Alliance, Ohio 1956*

How Once We Looked

The world I experienced, as the 1940s slid into the 1950s and beyond

When I created a snapshot of my four-year old sister, I had no idea that I would be pursuing photography as an avocation, let alone a profession. Our mother did her best to expose us to the arts, even enrolling me in classes with adults at a local art center. As a youngster, I knew I wasn't good enough at painting.

But I did have a sense of composition, and a science teacher at State Street Junior High School, Miss Ayers, had set up a small darkroom and invited me to use it. I became enamored of photography. I was living in a Rust Belt town in Ohio where I didn't belong, in the 1950s. What to do when you don't fit in? In my teen years, I hid behind a camera.

My swords and shields as I moved on to high school began with the Speed Graphics assigned in photography class. I became a local treasure, winning in contests but with a whole lot to learn and a vital need to grow myself up.

It took grit, I now realize, to escape the confines both of a family business and of the values of my community. But all I knew then was that I had an enthusiasm that I must explore. It eventually led to a profession. Photographing with intuition became the foundation of my work.

Told today that my files are a treasure trove, I'm going back into the archives to see what I saw long ago. First up is this sampling of my documentary photography, a nostalgic look covering a span of years. I've selected images that seem memorable, from the perspective of a life spent pursuing my passion.

— Michael Philip Manheim

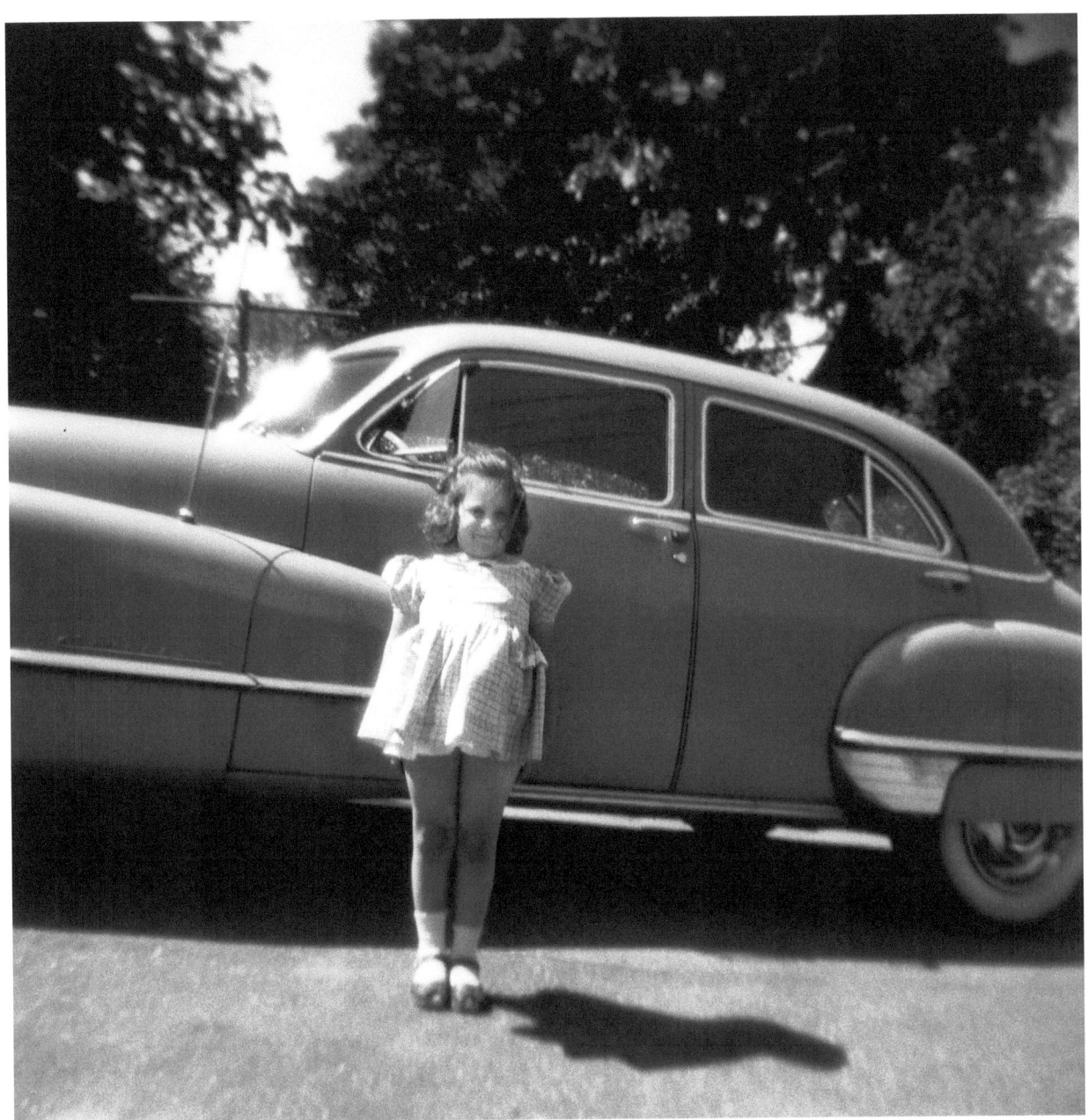

Little Sister *Alliance, Ohio 1947*

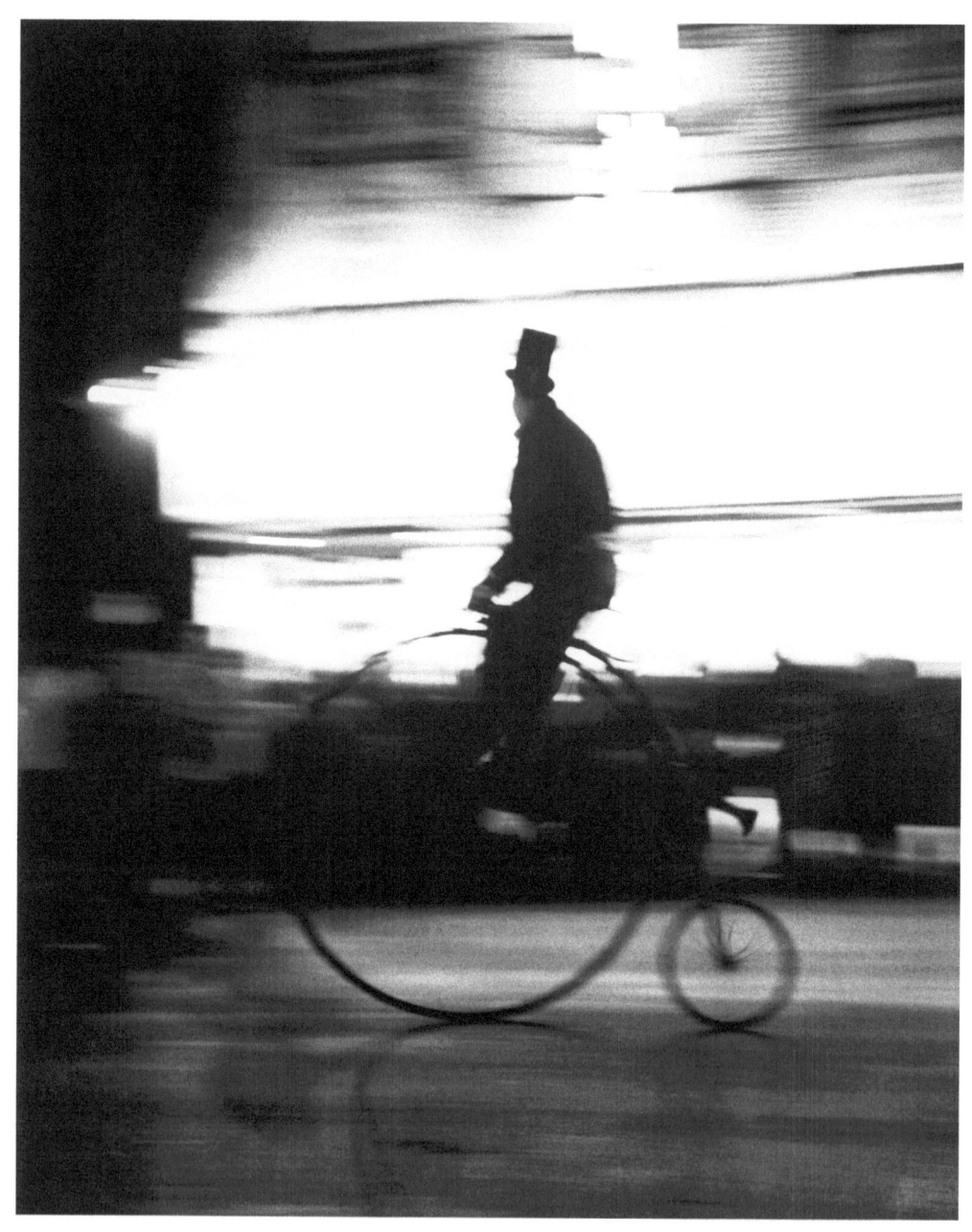

The Cyclist *Alliance, Ohio 1955*

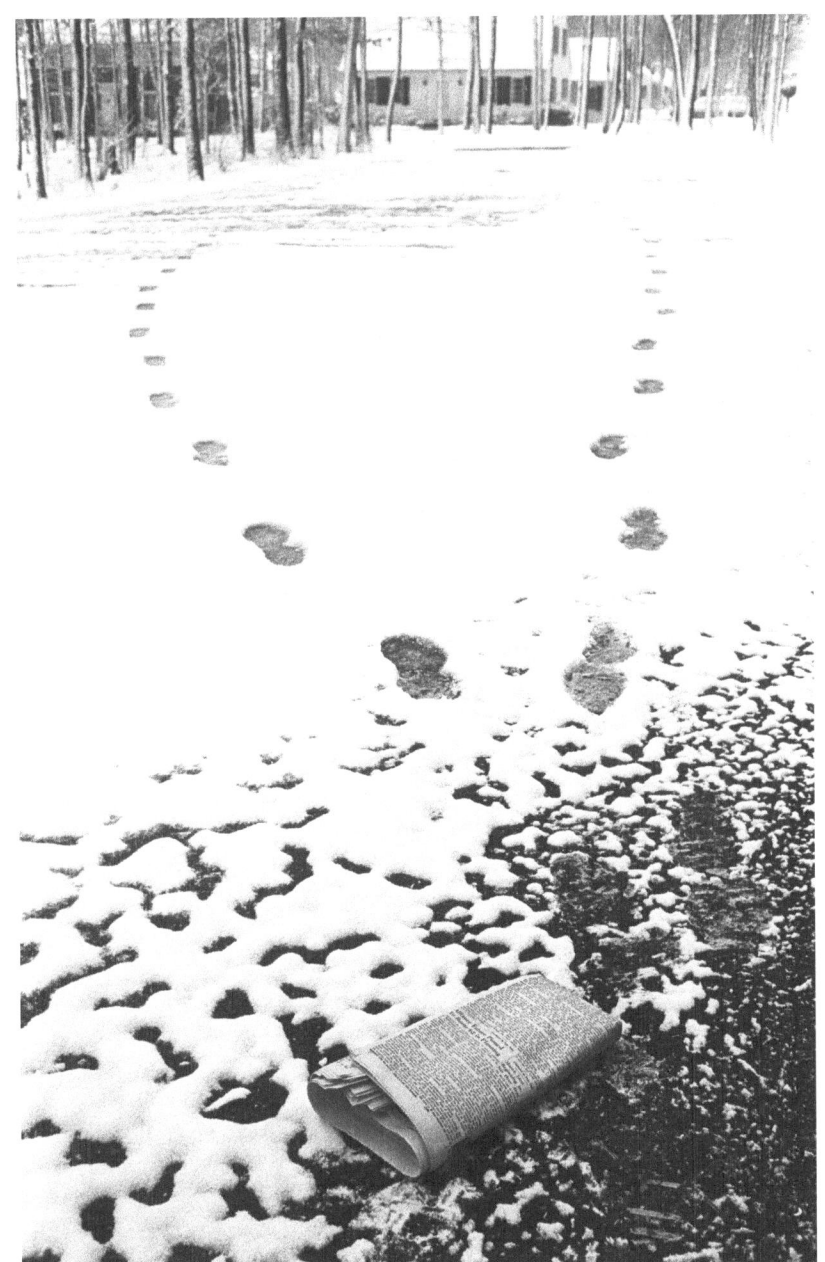

Morning Newspaper *Alliance, Ohio 1956*

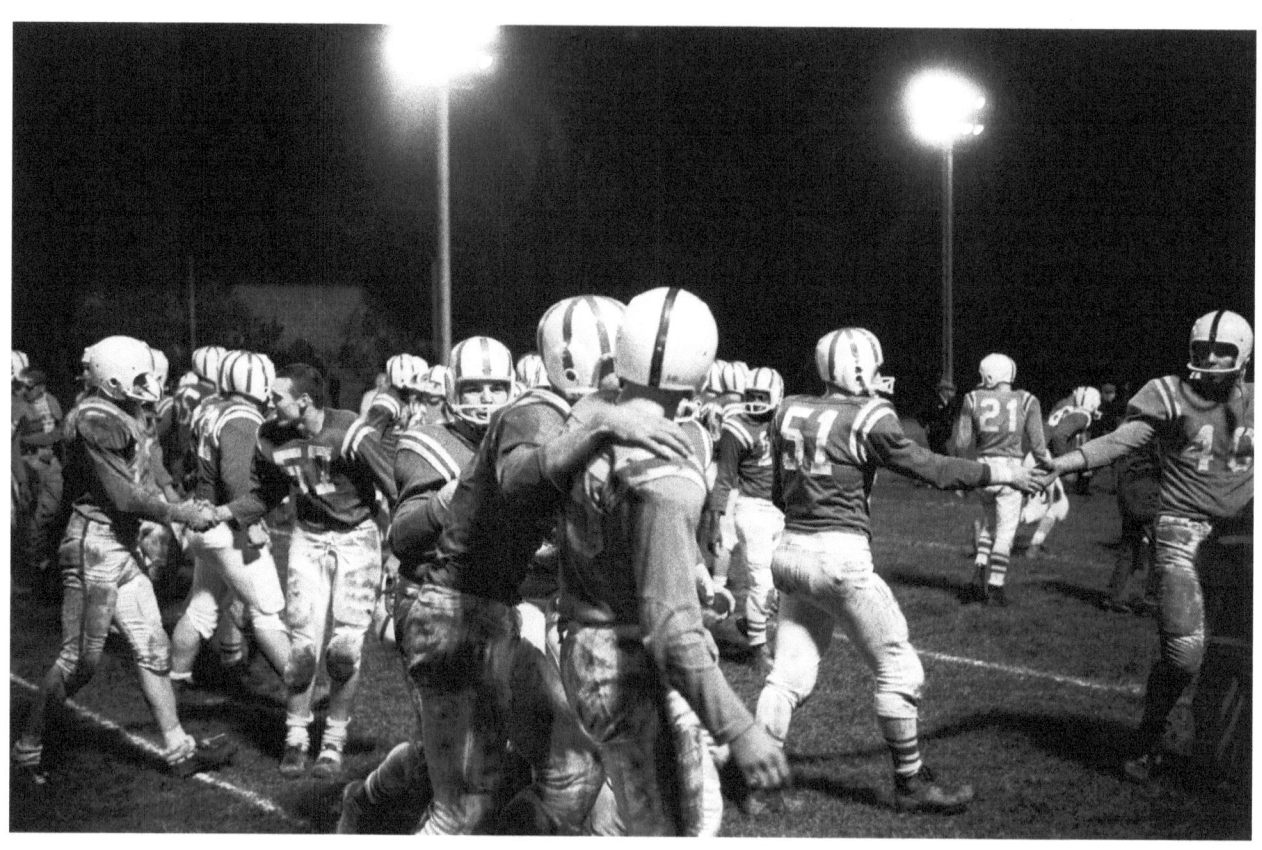

Sports Shake *Alliance, Ohio 1957*

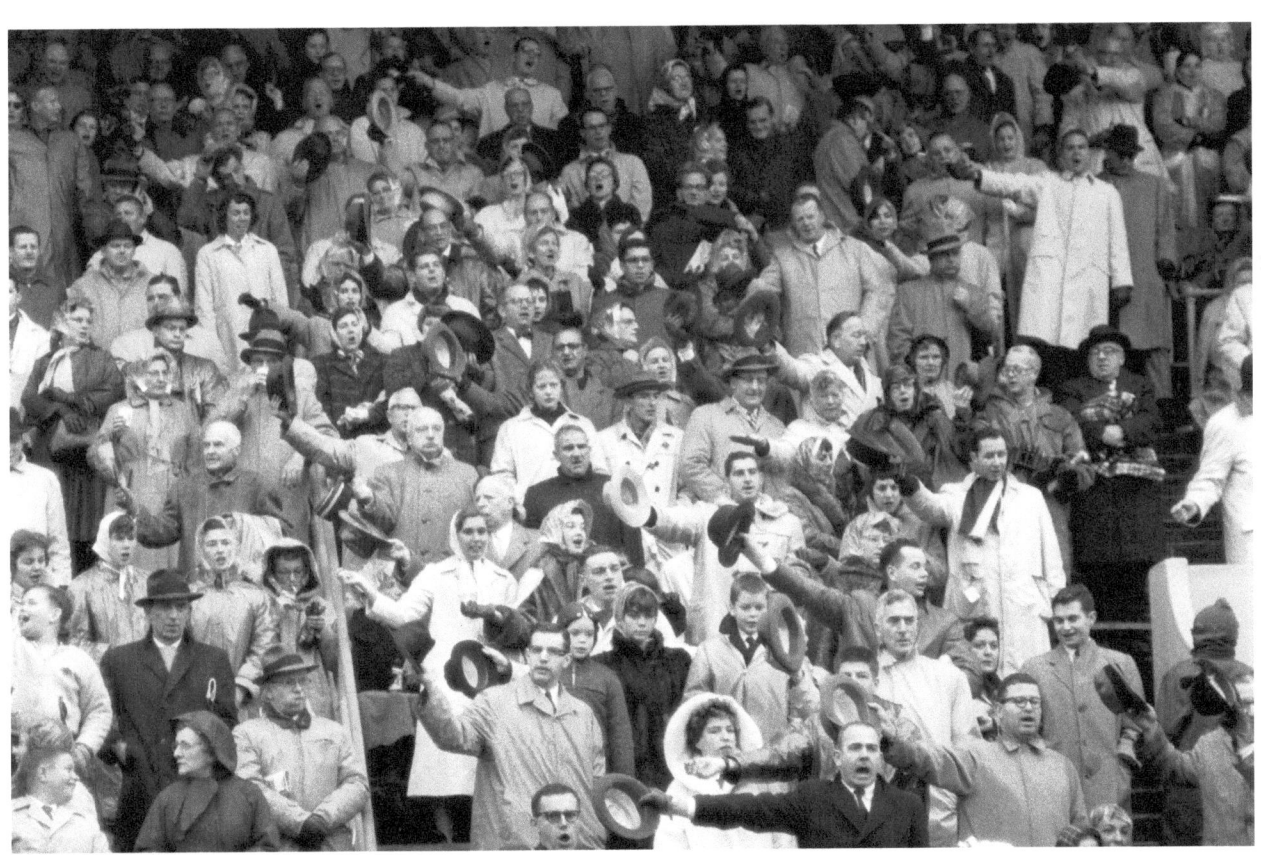

Alma Mater *Philadelphia, Pennsylvania 1958*

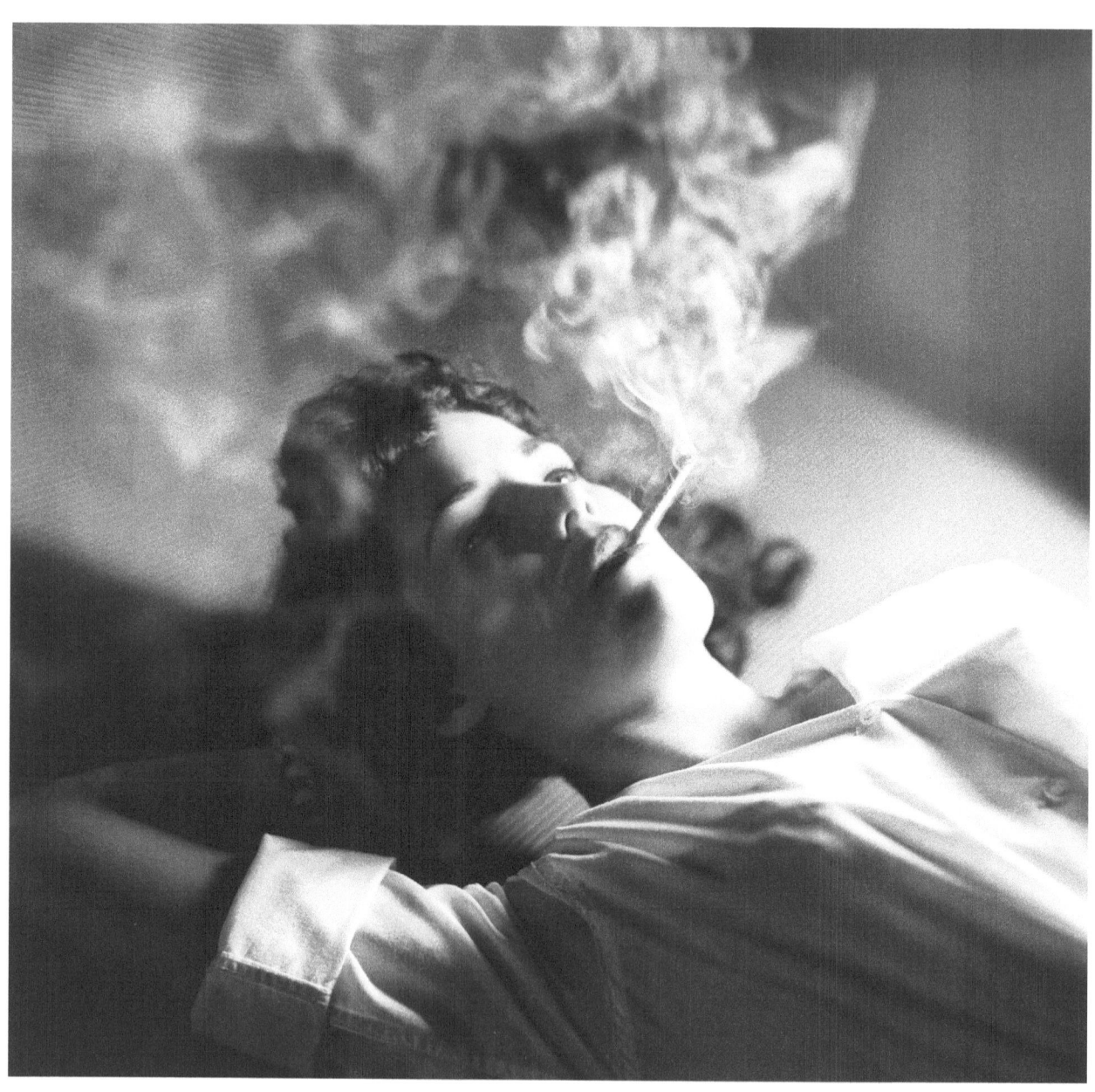

Girl Smoking *Alliance, Ohio 1959*

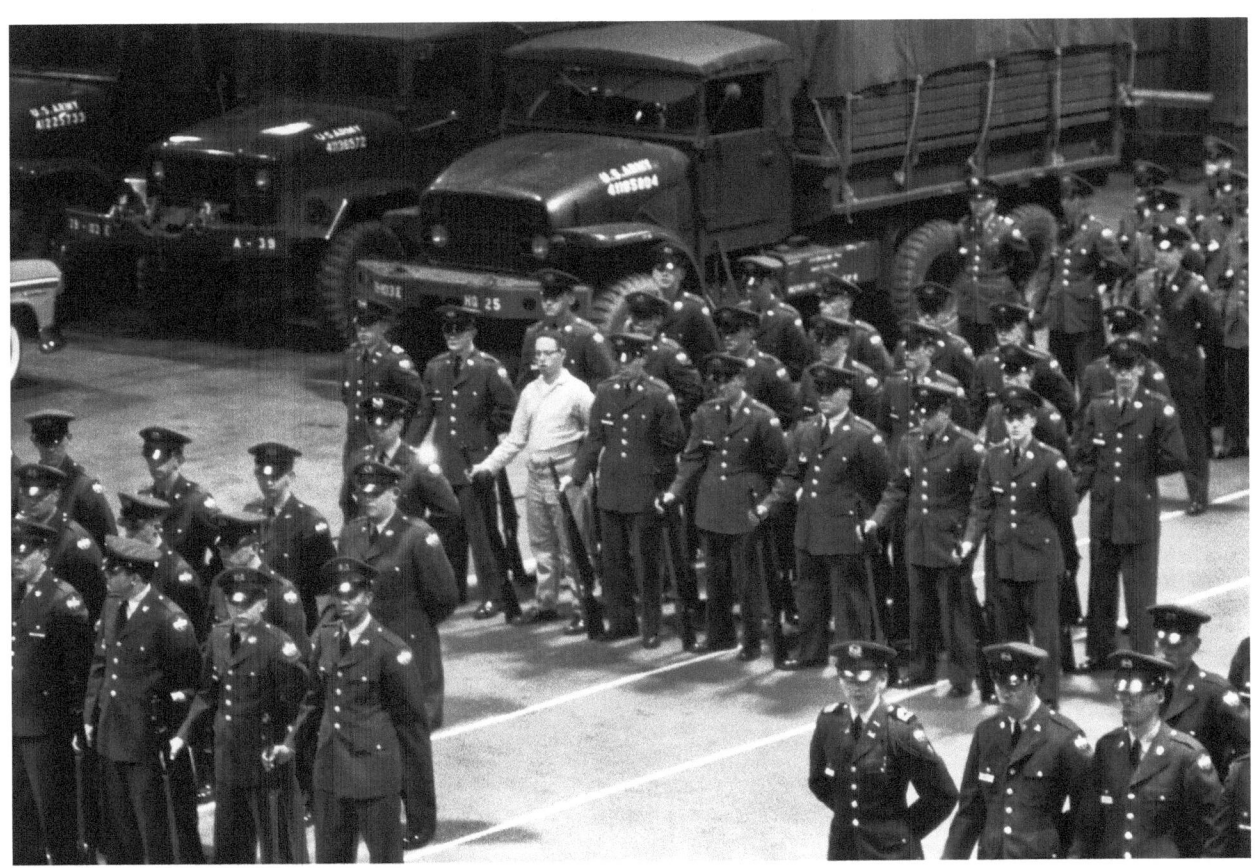

Sore Thumb *Philadelphia, PA 1959*

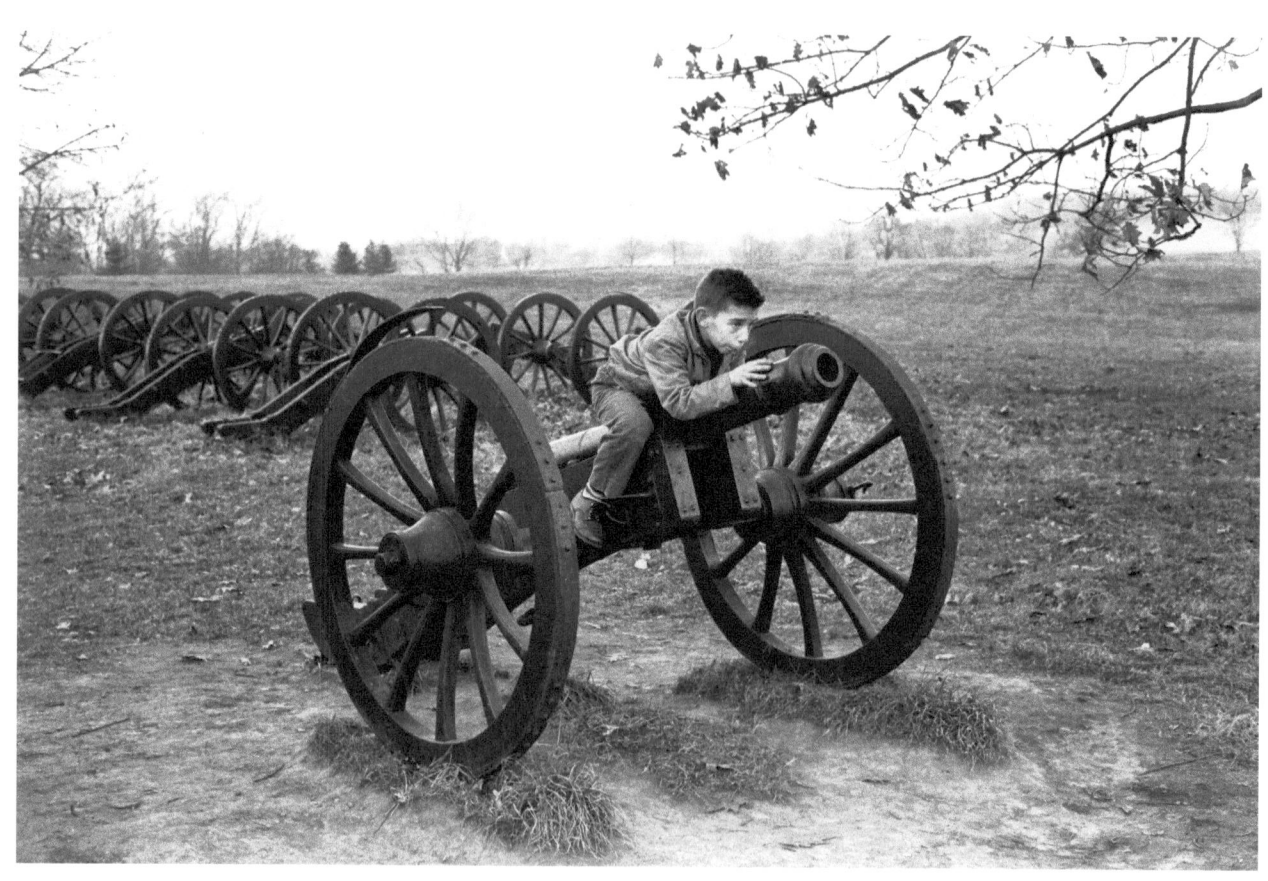

Reverie *Valley Forge, Pennsylvania 1961*

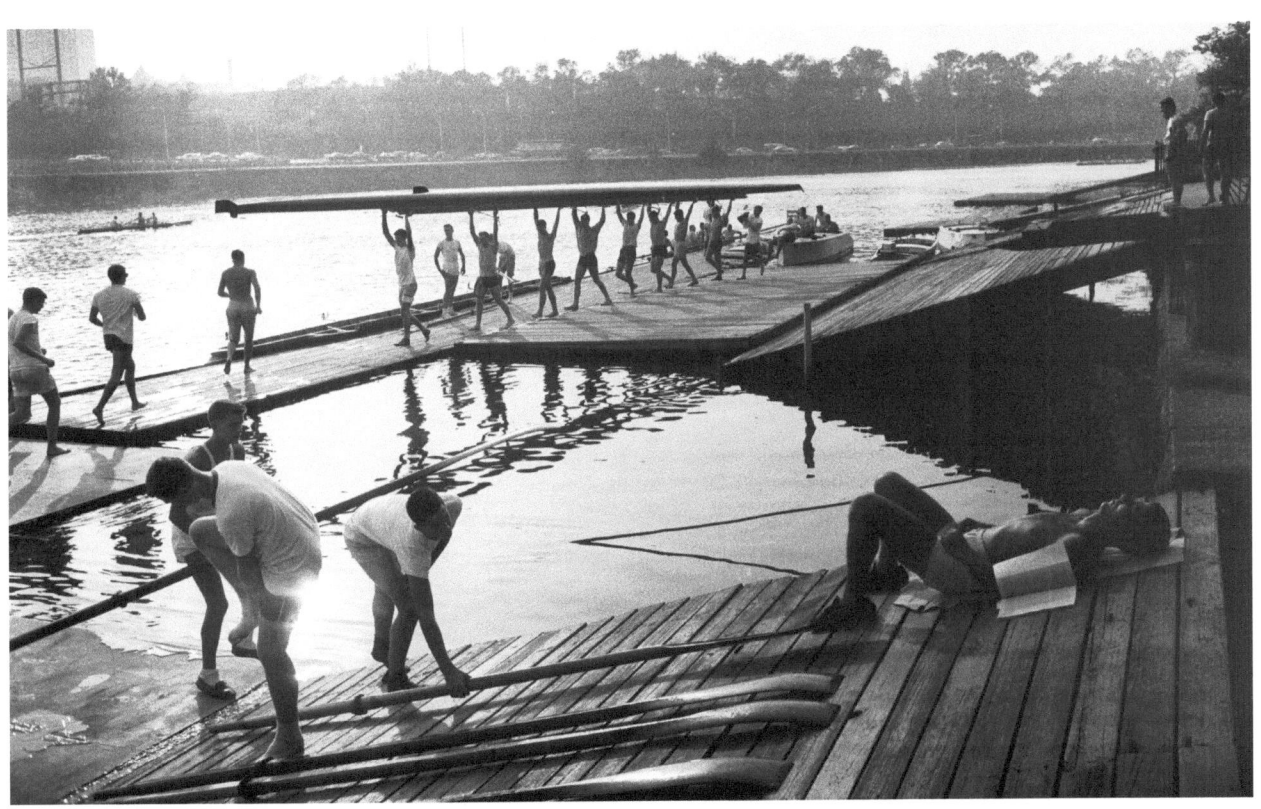

Launch *Philadelphia, Pennsylvania 1961*

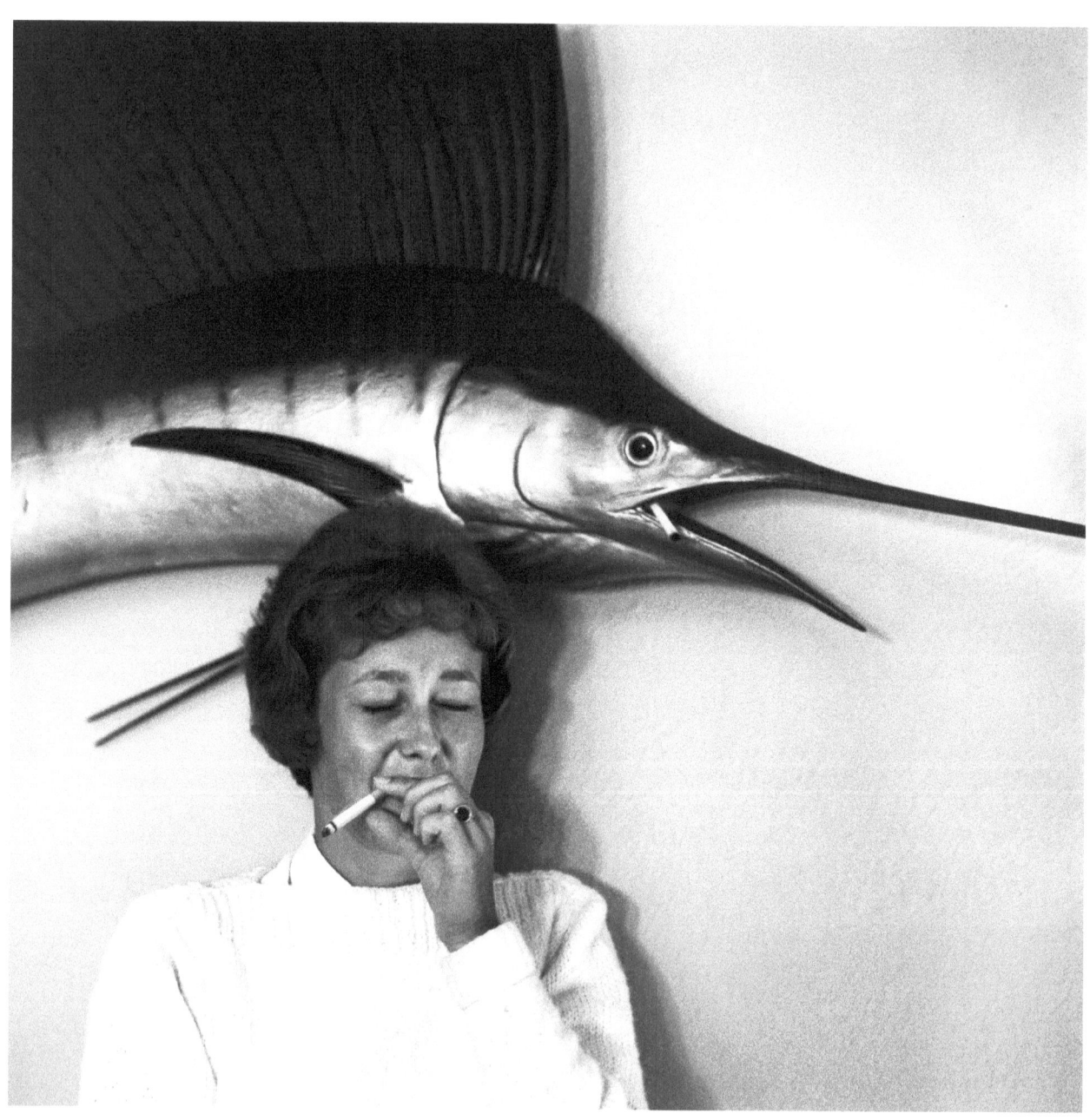

Twin Smokes *Ocean City, New Jersey 1961*

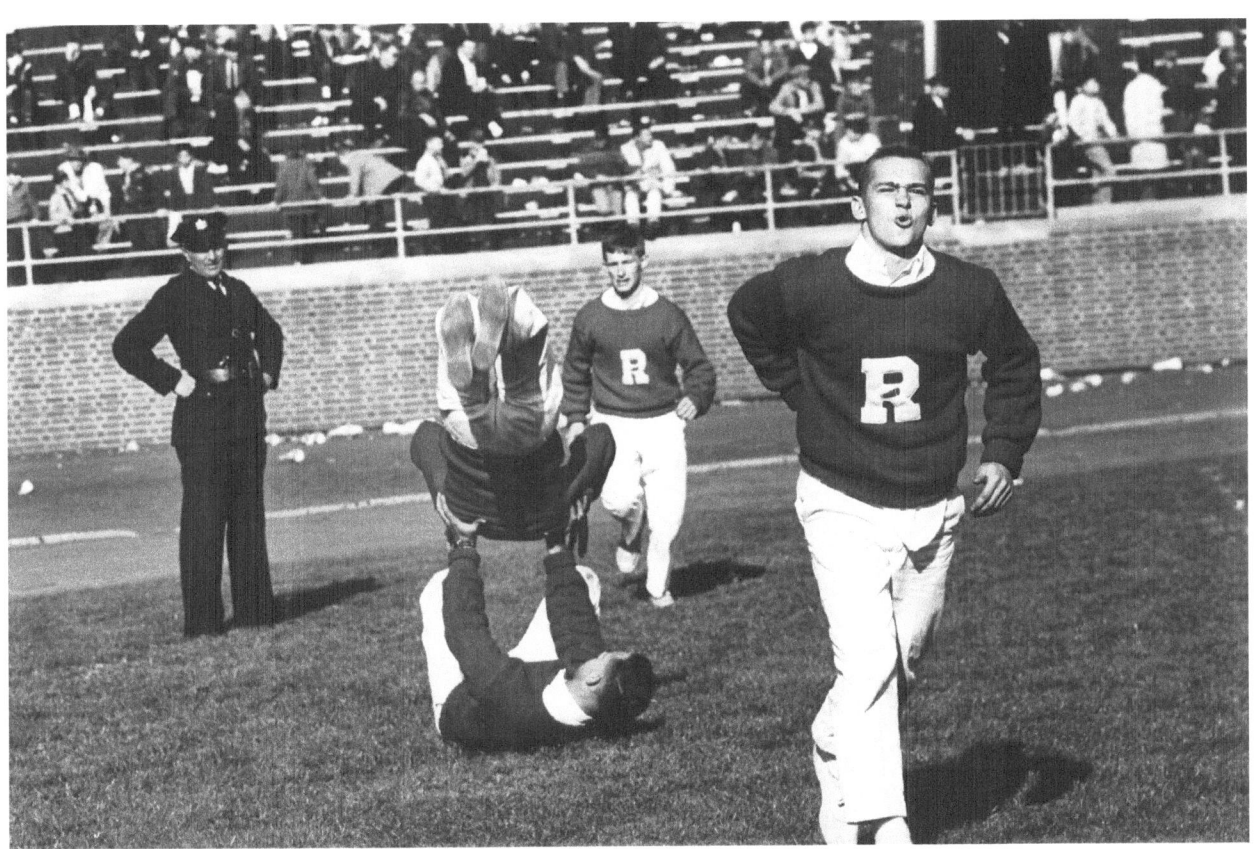

Fumble Tumble *Philadelphia, Pennsylvania 1961*

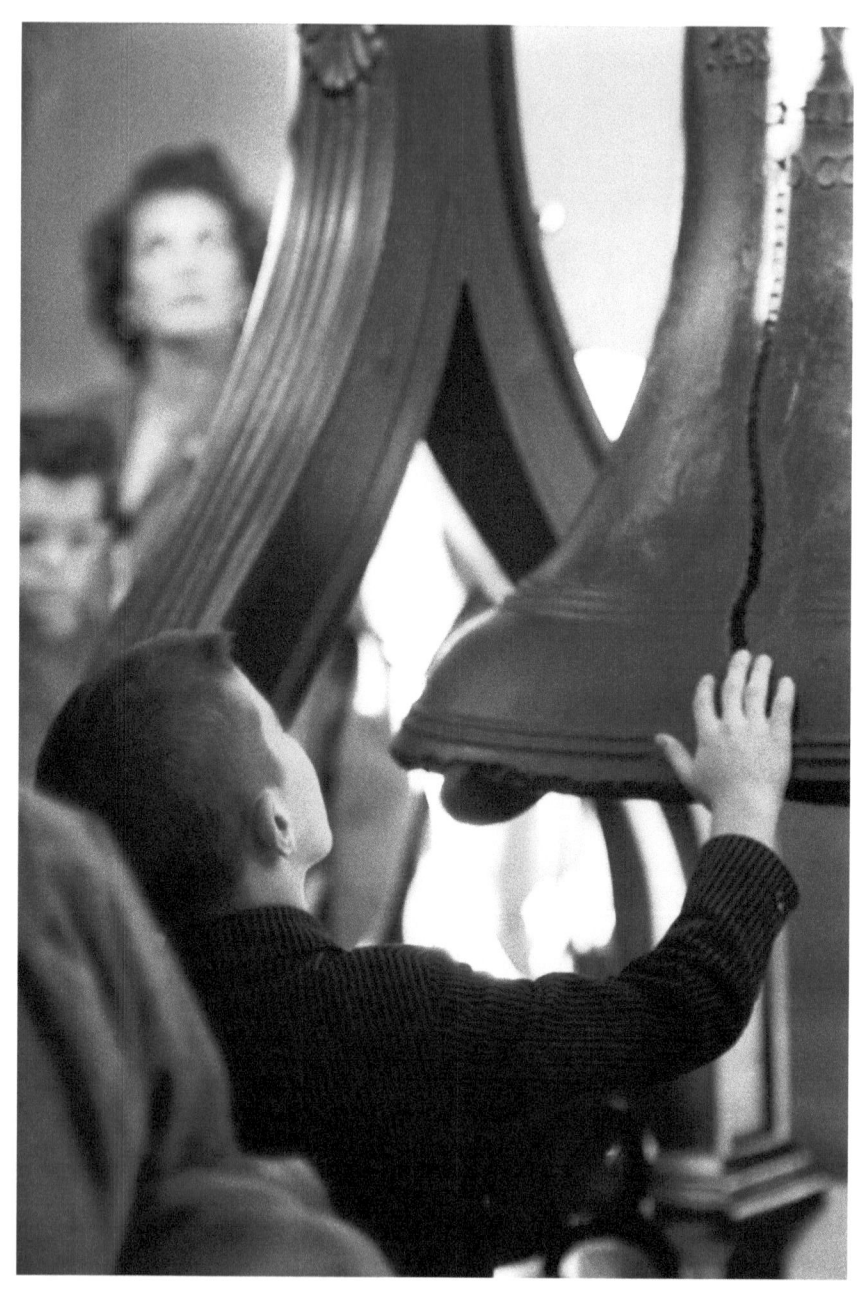

Touch *Philadelphia, Pennsylvania 1962*

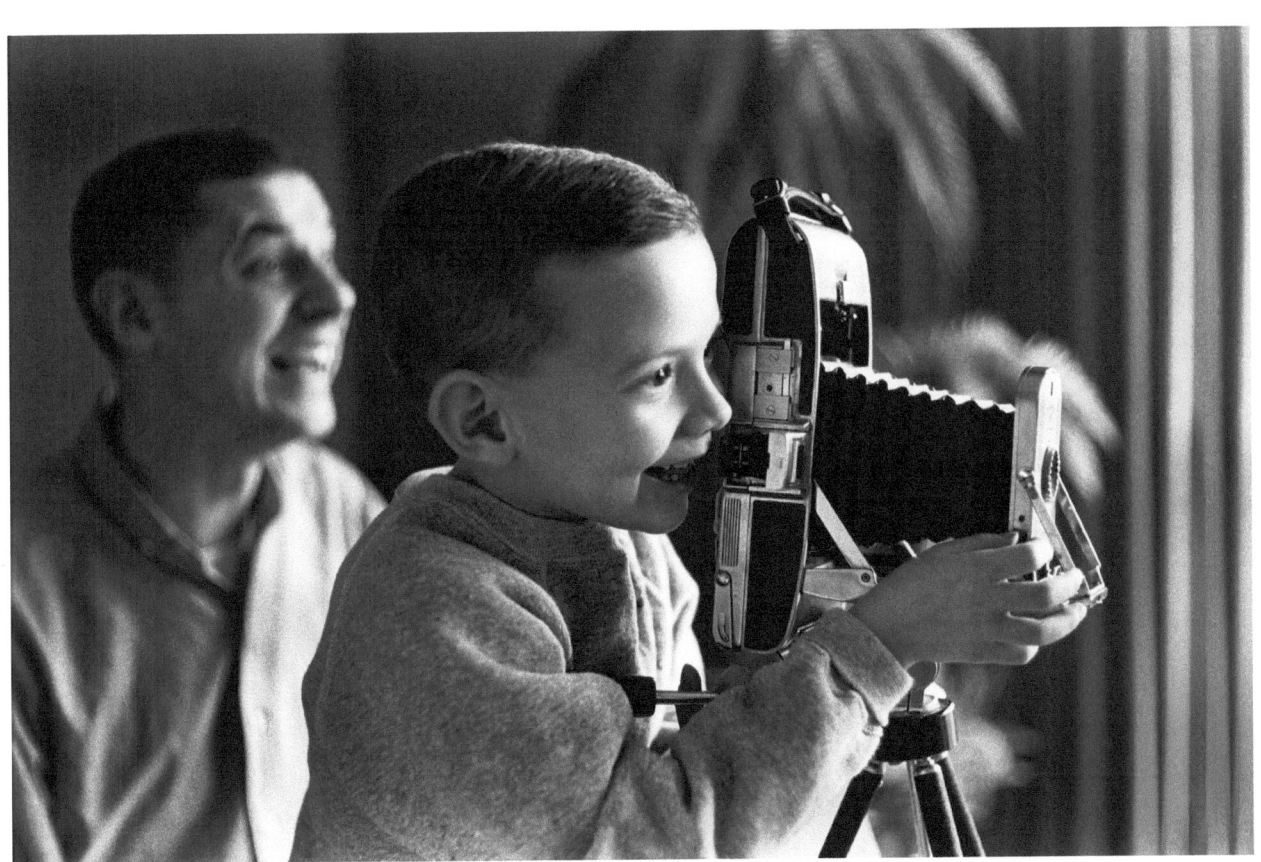

Small Shot *Canton, Ohio 1965*

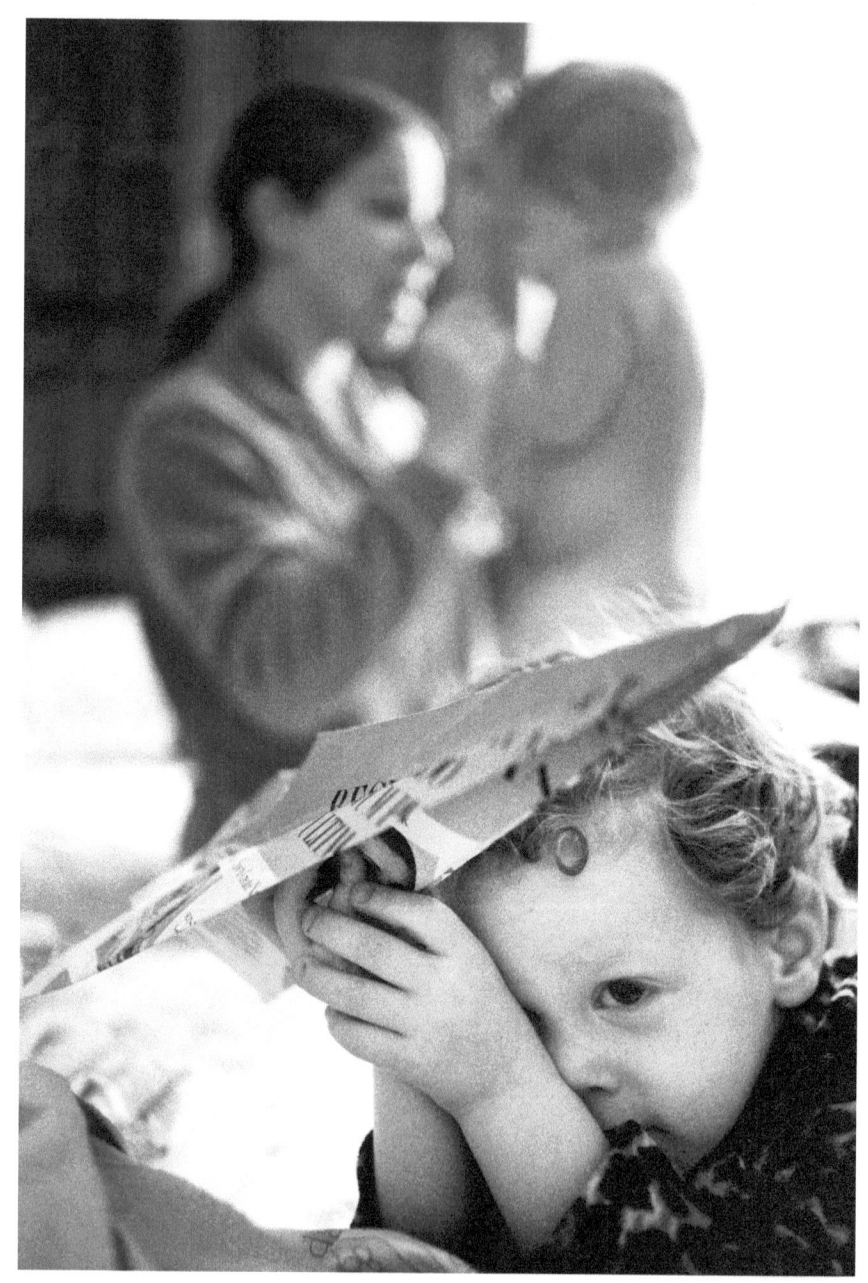

Siblings *Marblehead, Massachusetts 1969*

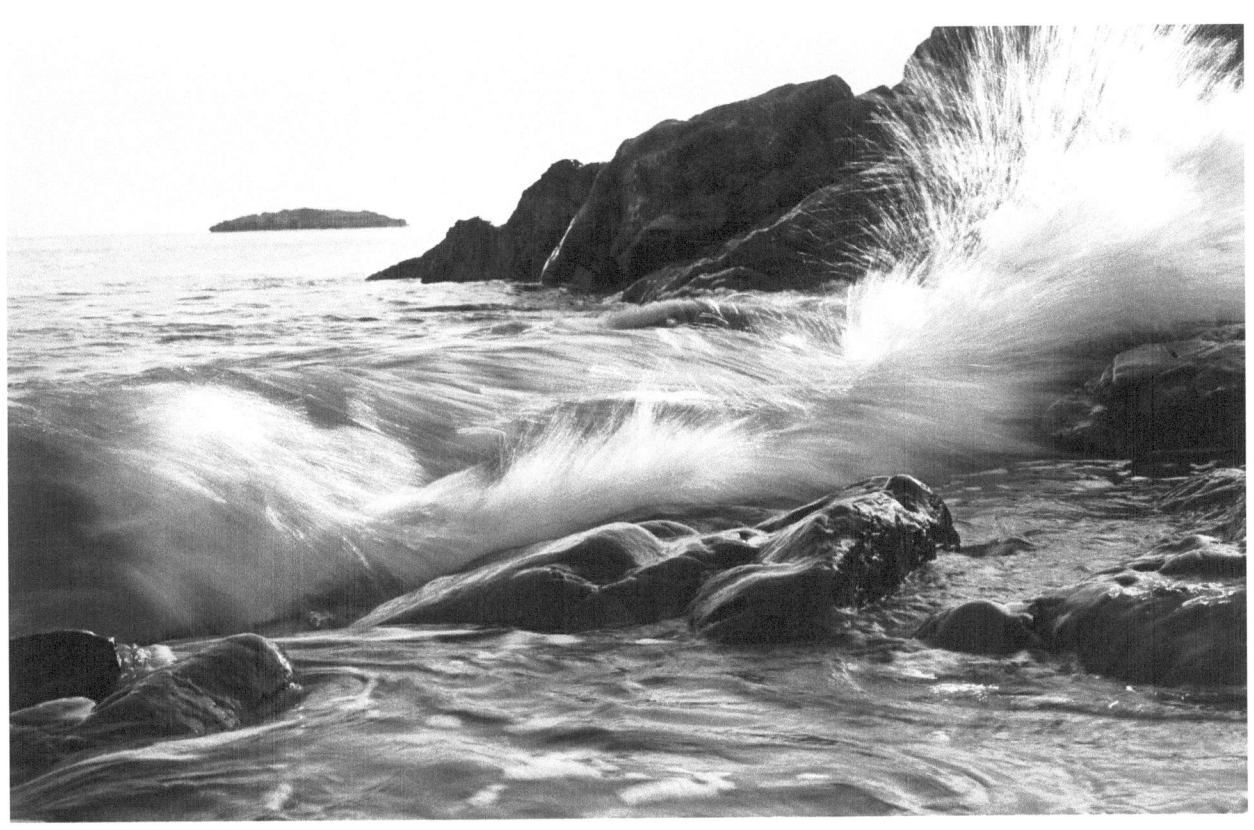

Breaking Wave *Marblehead, Massachusetts 1972*

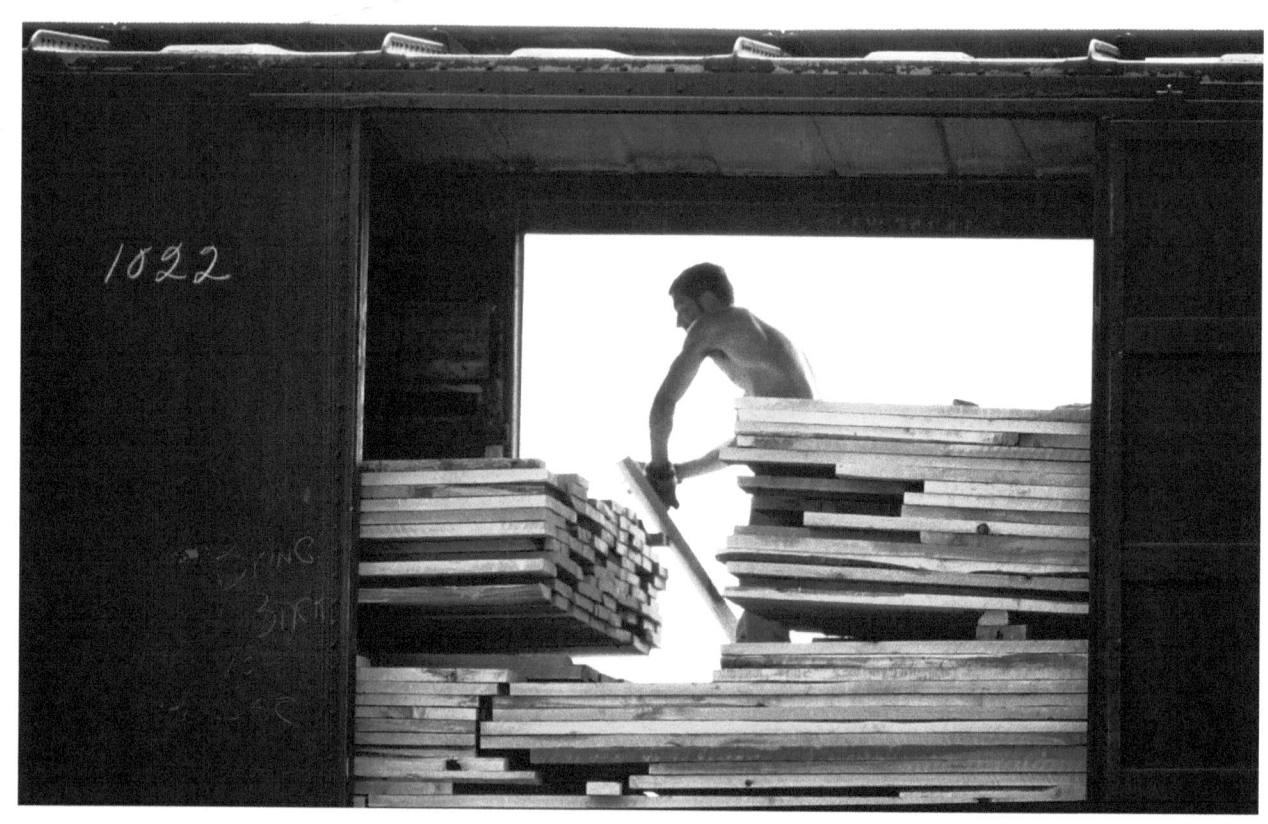

Lumber Loading *Hartville, Ohio 1972*

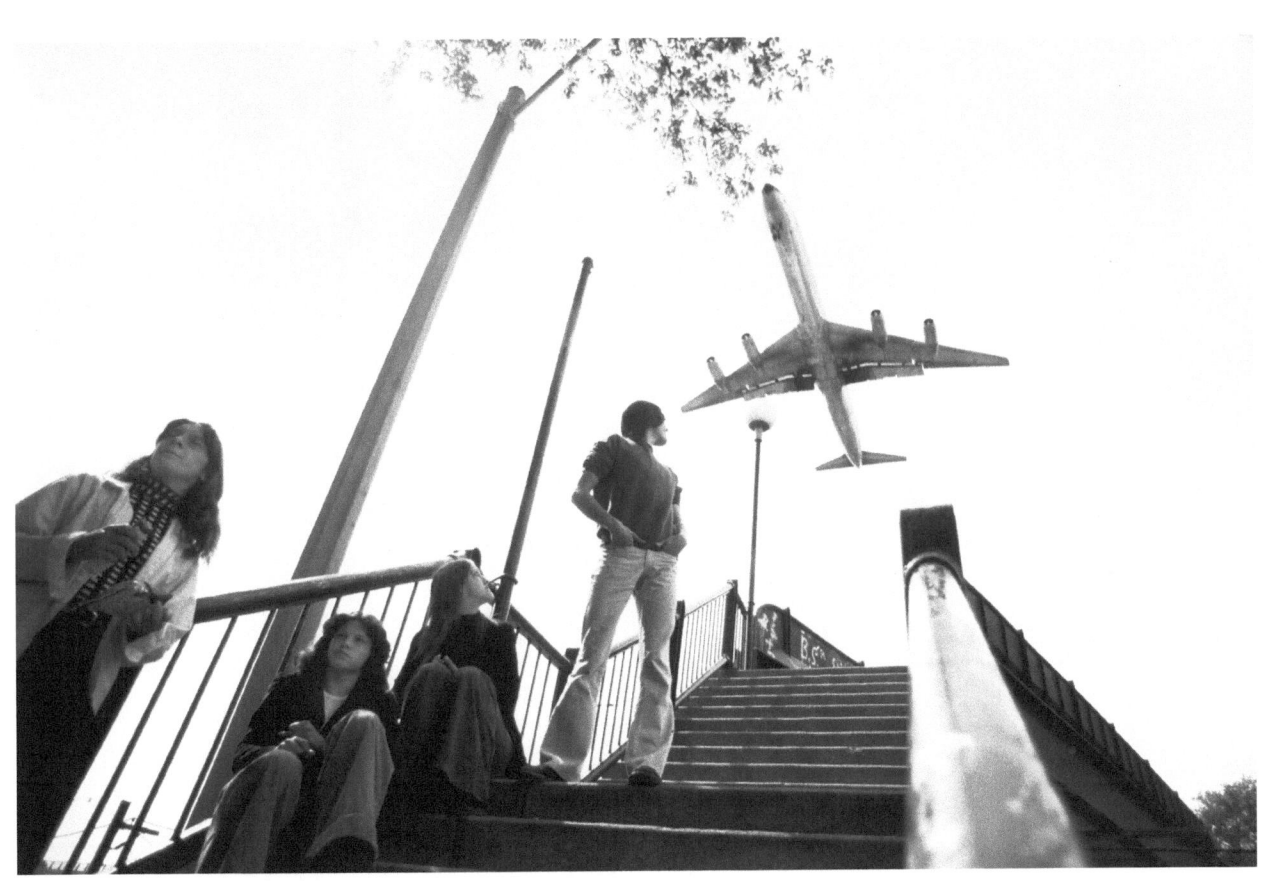

Landing at Logan *East Boston, Massachusetts 1973*

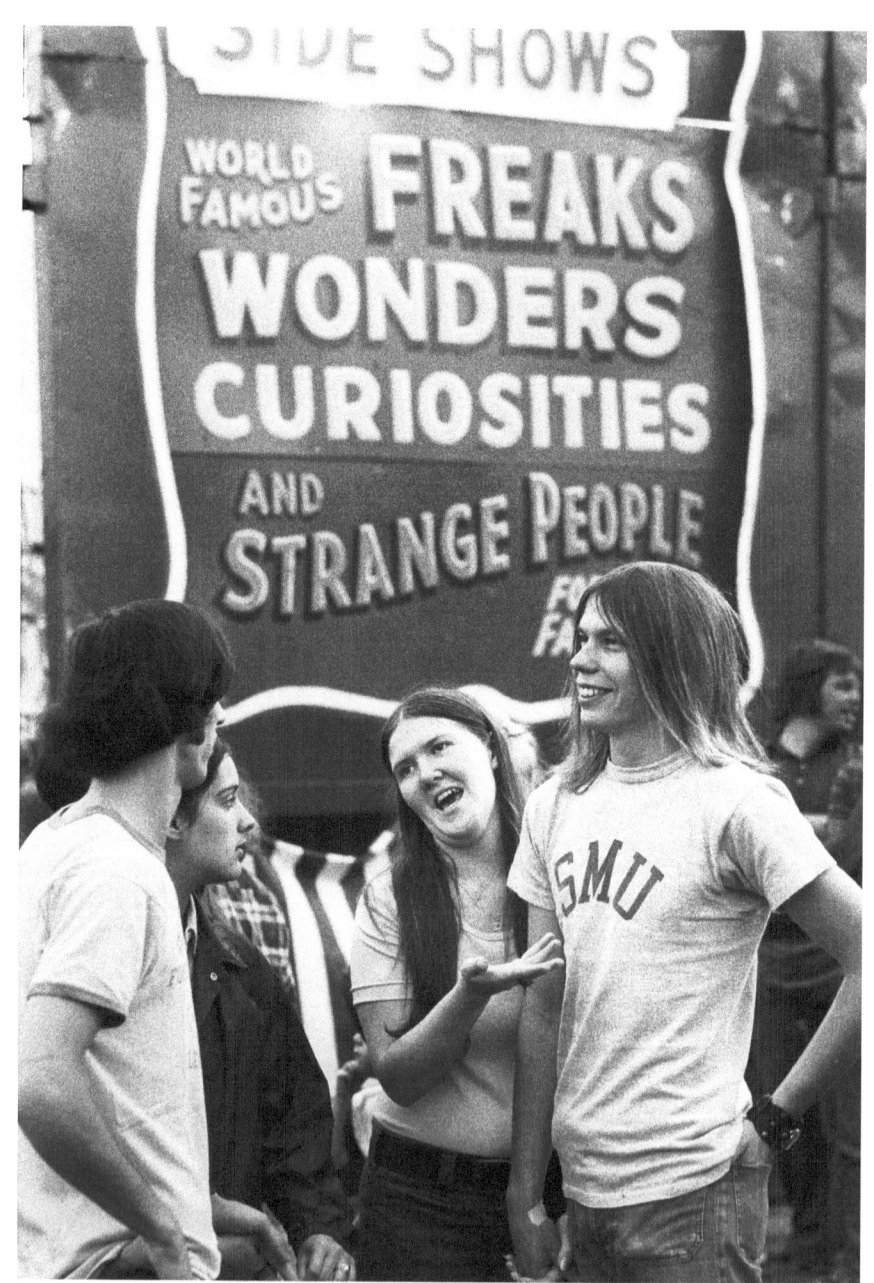

Freaks *Fall River, Massachusetts 1973*

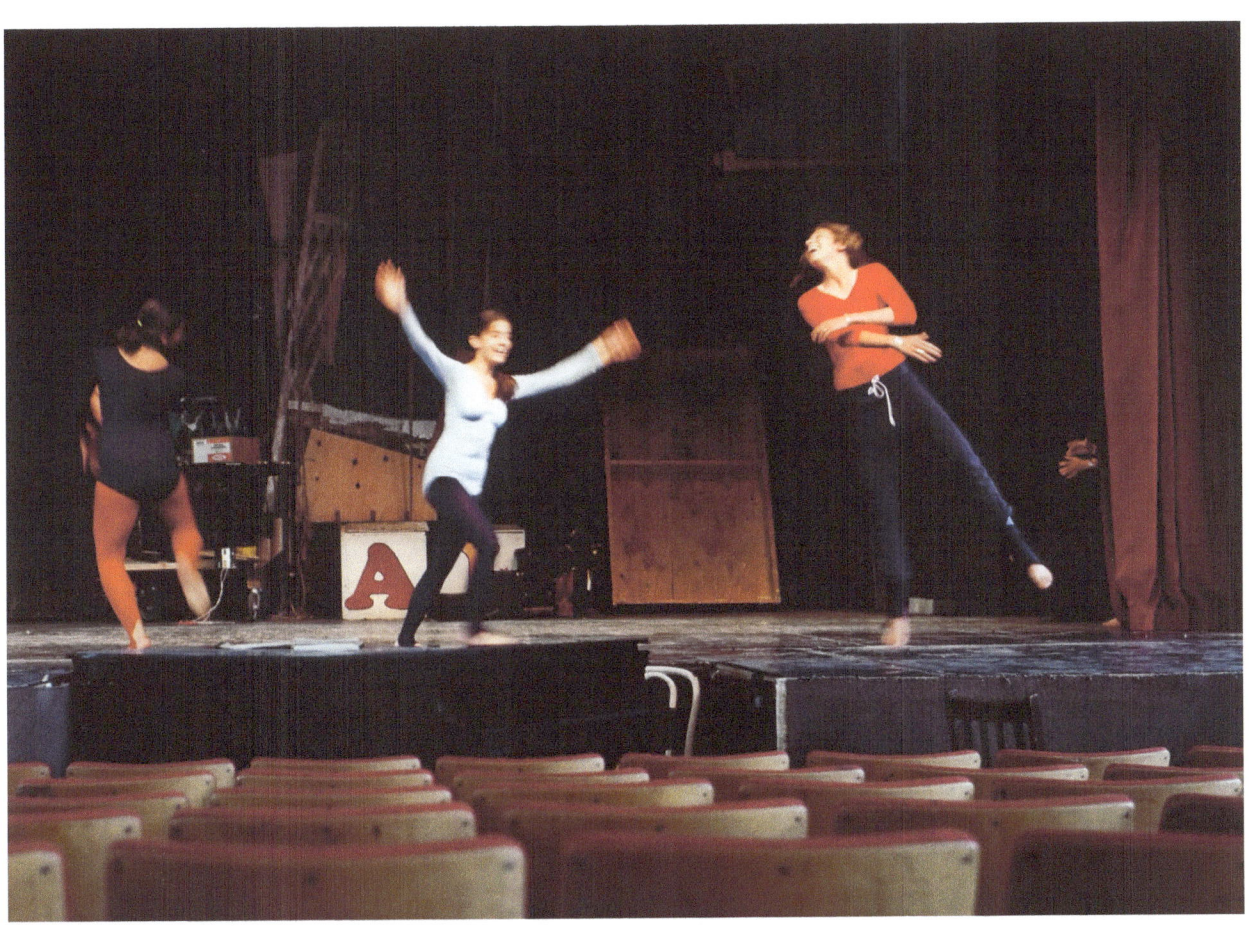

Exuberant Dancers *Pomfret, Connecticut 1977*

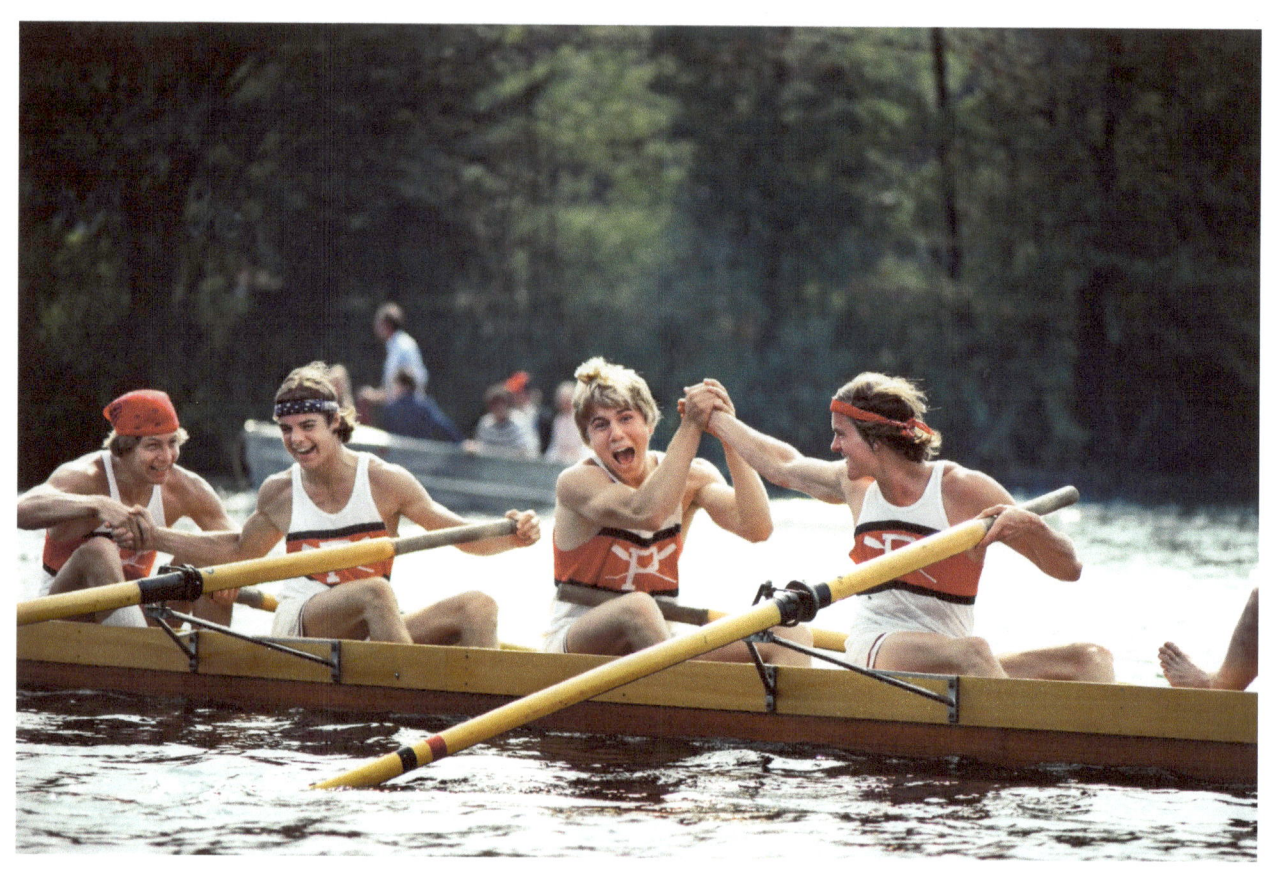

Winning Crew *Pomfret, Connecticut 1977*

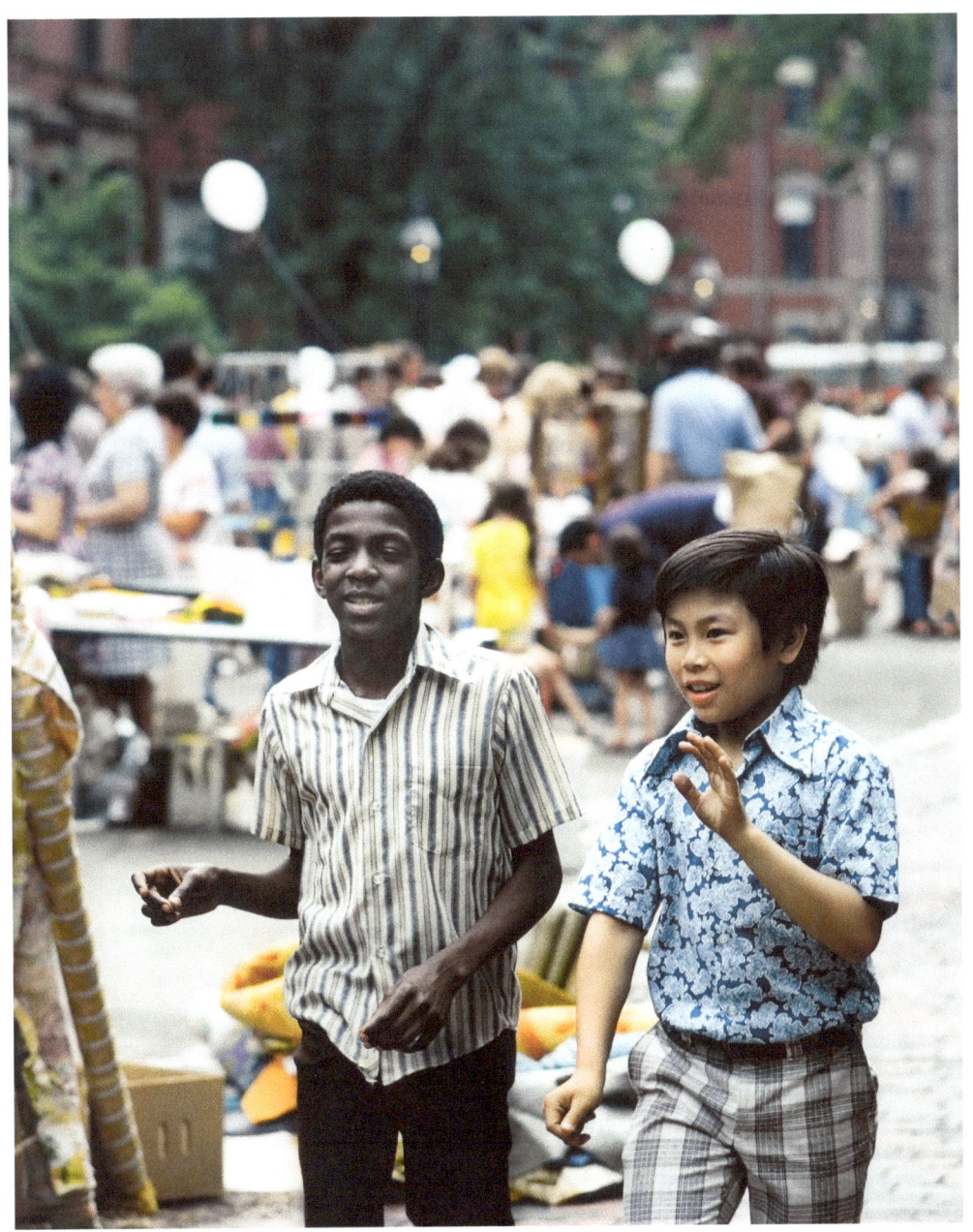

Boys Click *Boston, Massachusetts 1975*

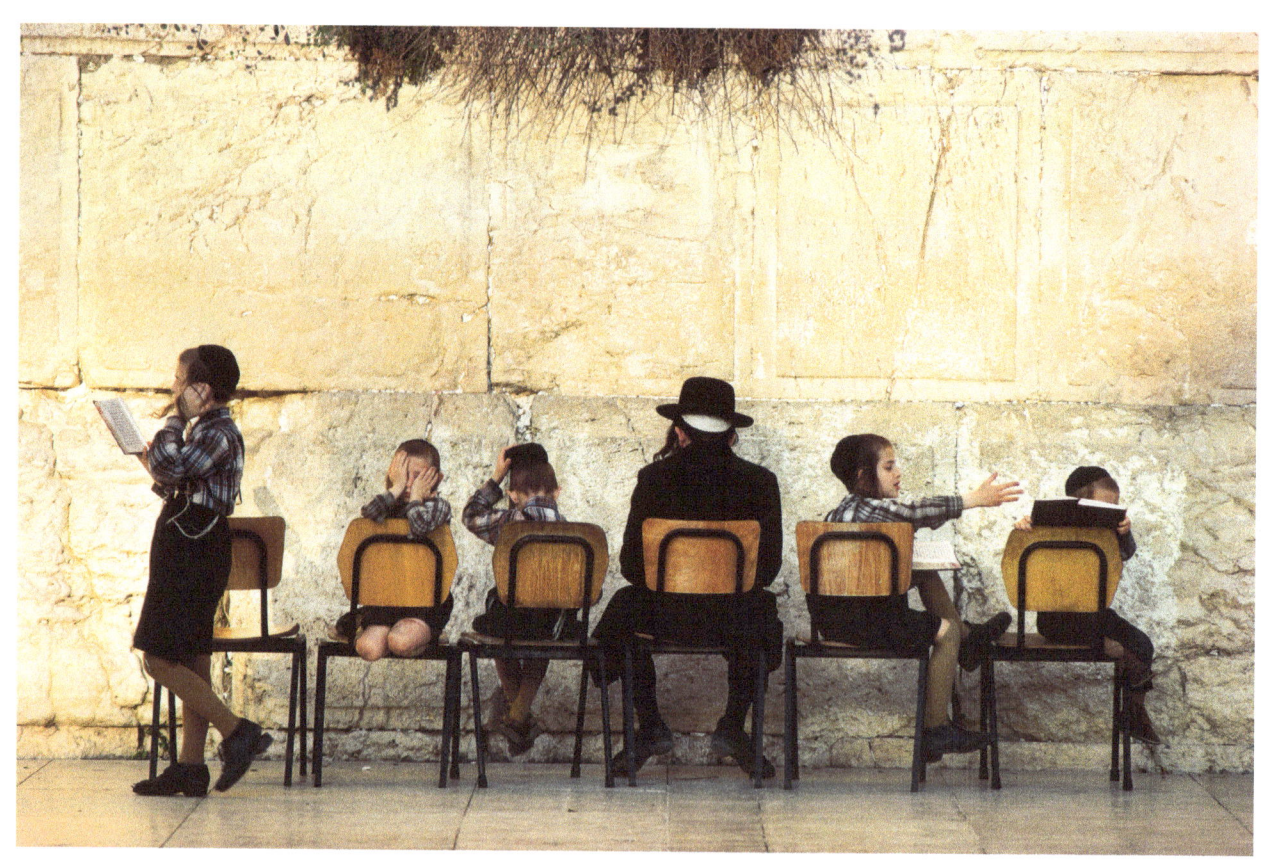

Boys at the Wall *Jerusalem, Israel 1980*

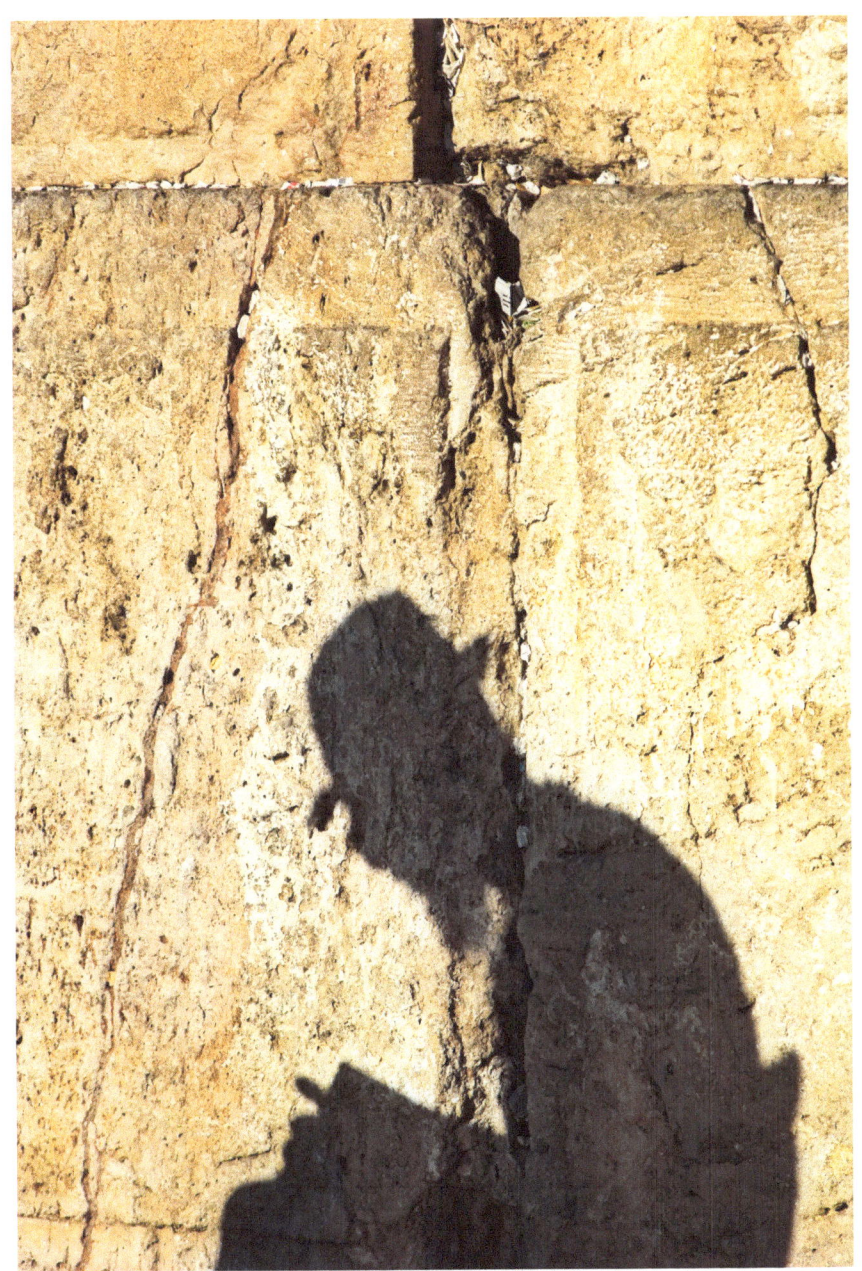

Shadow on the Wall *Jerusalem, Israel 1980*

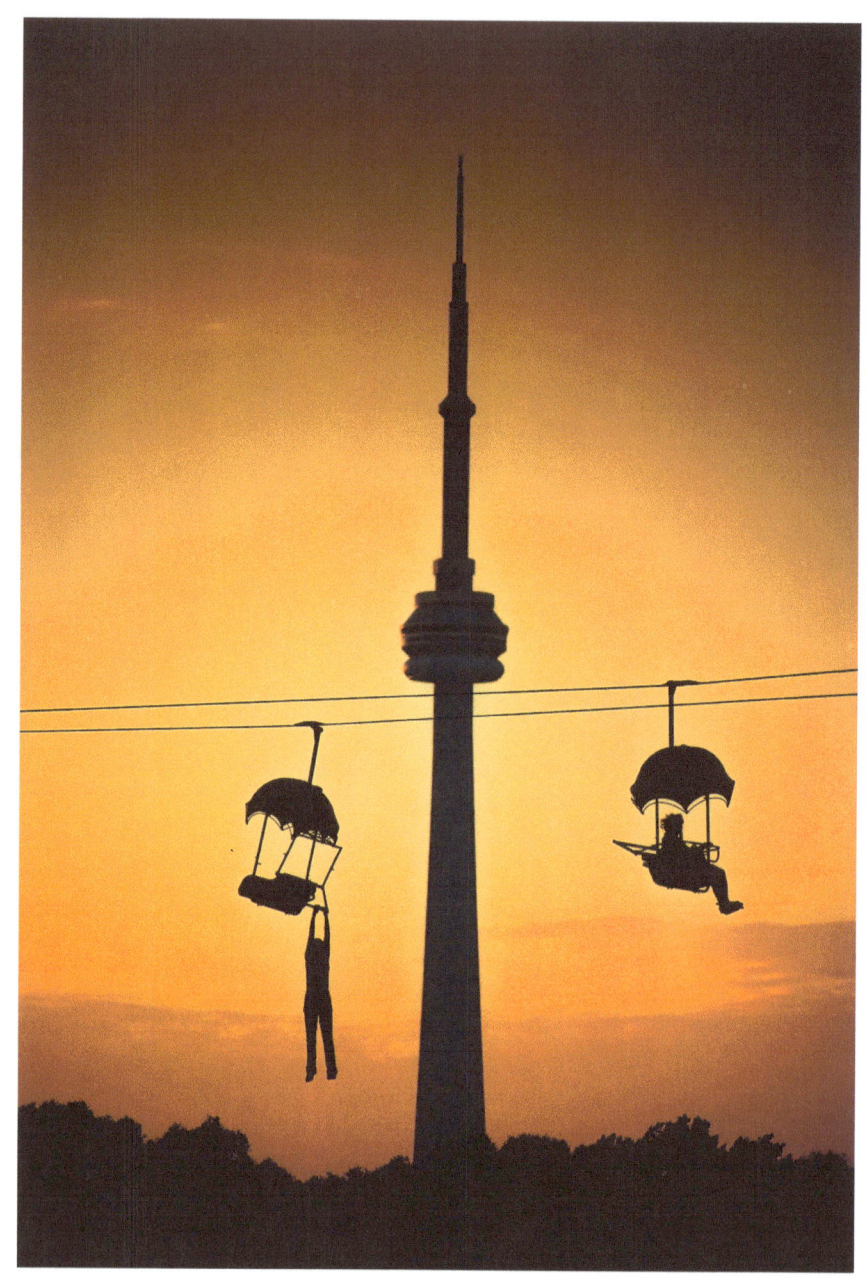

Hanging Out *Toronto Ontario, Canada 1976*

IMAGE INSIGHTS

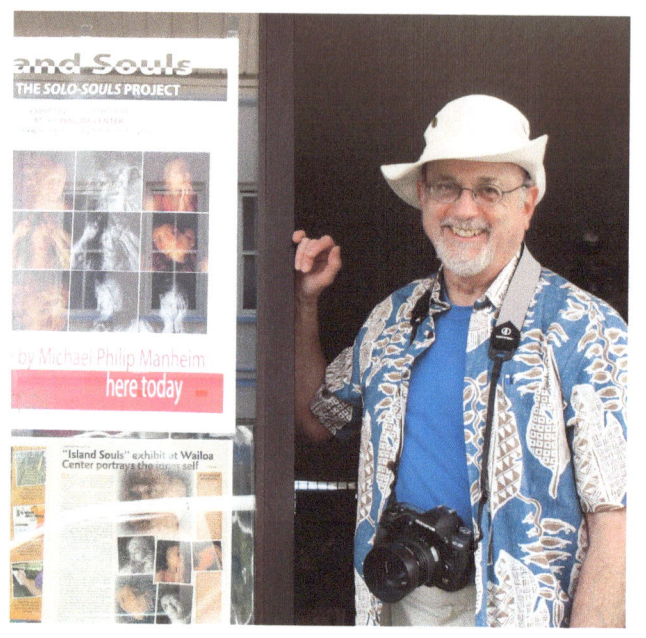

Michael Philip Manheim

Manheim is widely recognized both for his documentary and for his innovative multiple exposure photographs. Both categories encompass images that promote feelings. Most celebrate human emotion as a primal link that unifies all of humankind.

Michael Philip Manheim's photography has been exhibited throughout the United States and internationally, in over 20 solo exhibitions and 30 group shows. His work has been featured extensively online, as well as in hundreds of books and magazines such as *Zoom* (U.S. and Italy), *Photographers International* (Taiwan), *La Fotografia* (Spain), and *Black and White Magazine* (U.S.).

Manheim's photographs are held in private as well as public collections including the Library of Congress, the International Photography Hall of Fame, the National Archives, the Danforth Museum of Art, and the Bates College Museum of Art.

www.ingramcontent.com/pod-product-compliance
Lightning Source LLC
Chambersburg PA
CBHW050908180526
45159CB00007B/2829